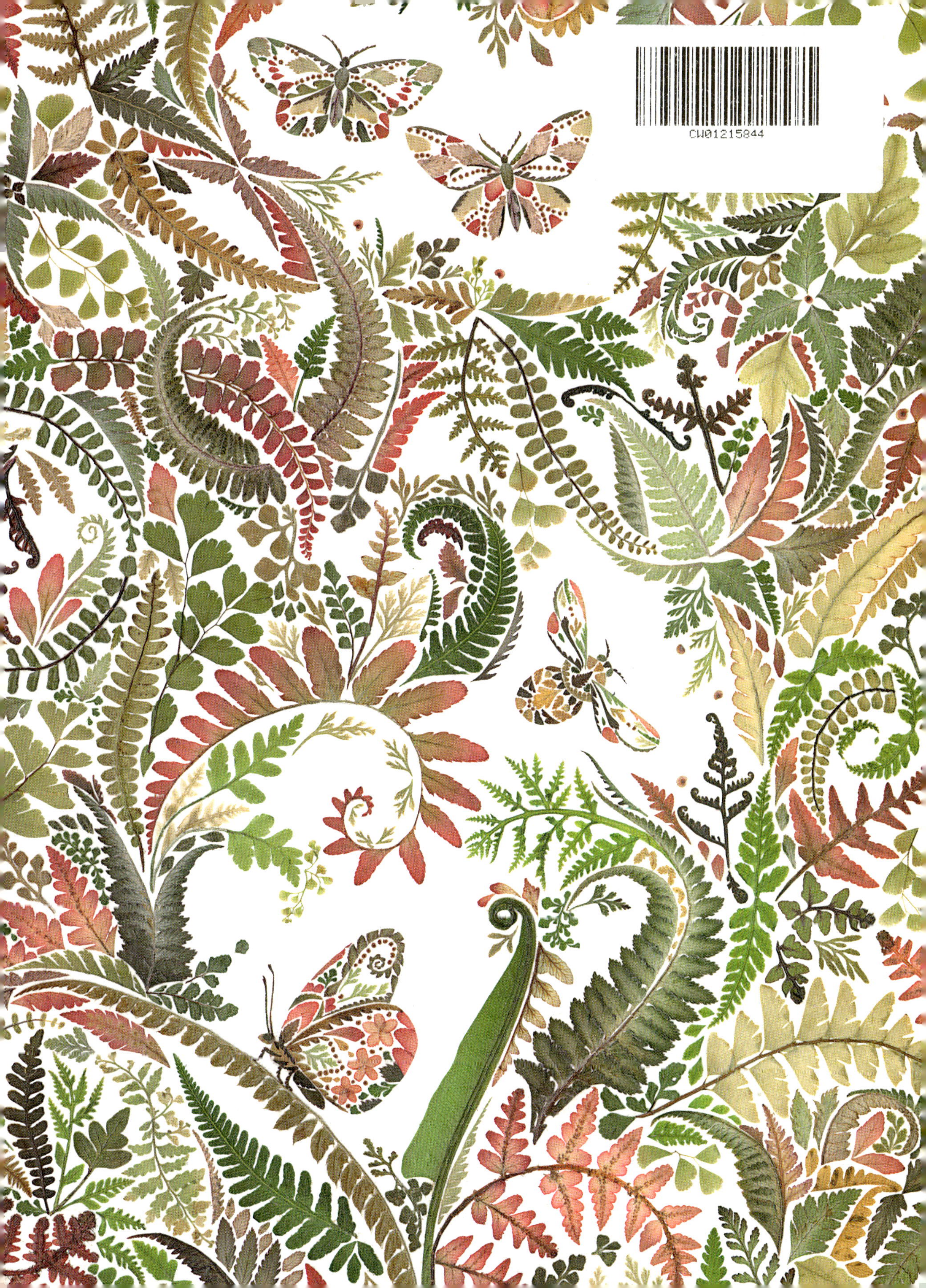

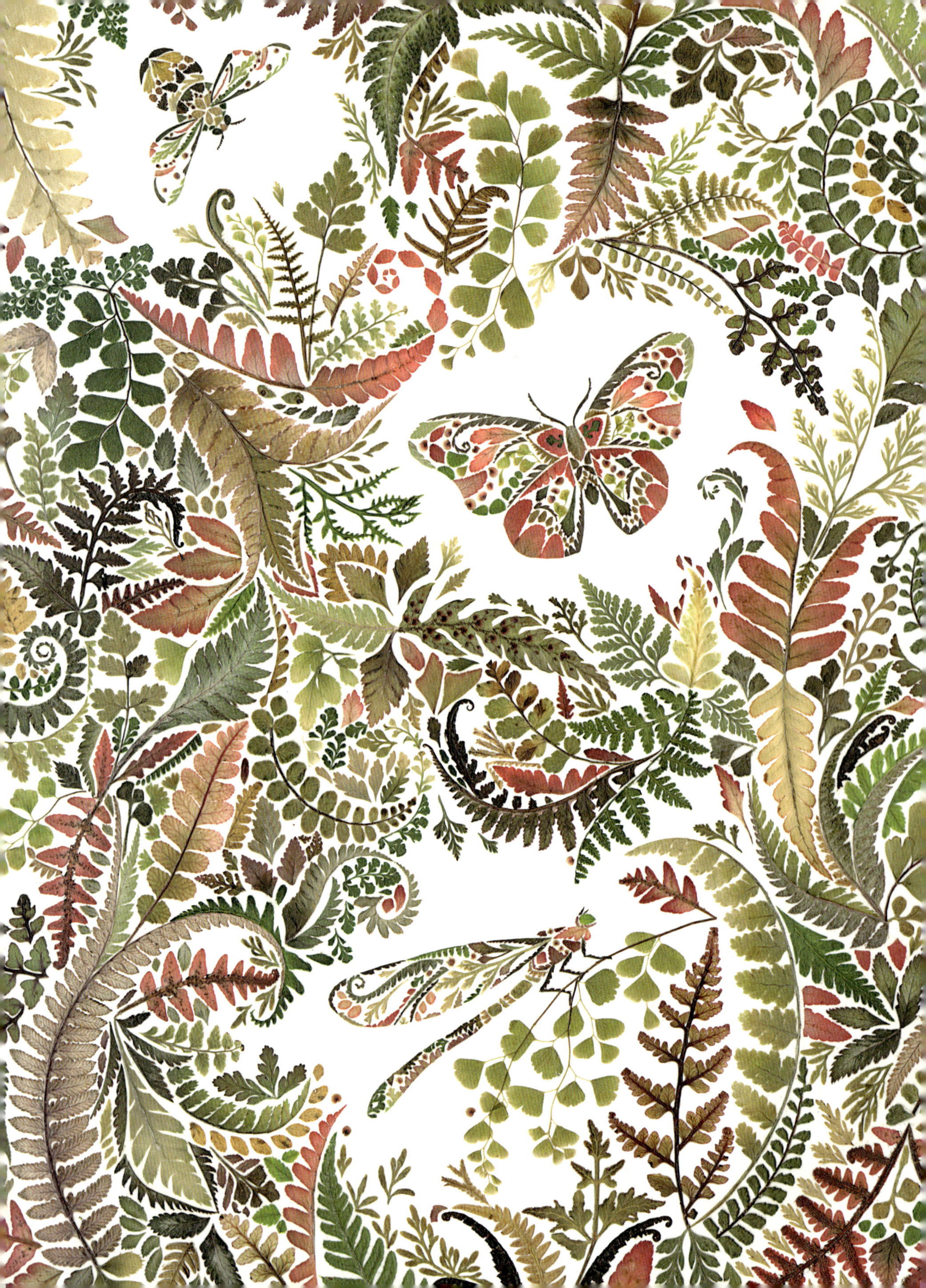

Helen Ahpornsiri's

a Year
in the
Wild

For my family, John, and little Helena – H.A.

BIG PICTURE PRESS

First published in the UK in 2018 by Big Picture Press,
an imprint of Kings Road Publishing,
part of the Bonnier Publishing Group,
The Plaza, 535 King's Road, London, SW10 0SZ
www.bonnierpublishing.com

Illustration copyright © 2018 by Helen Ahpornsiri
Text and design copyright © 2018 by The Templar Company Limited

1 3 5 7 9 10 8 6 4 2

All rights reserved

ISBN 978-1-78370-796-6

This book was typeset in Garton, Perpetua and Aristelle Script
The illustrations were created with petals and leaves

Designed by Nathalie Eyraud
Written and edited by Ruth Symons
Consultant: Camilla de la Bédoyère

Printed in Malaysia

Helen Ahpornsiri's
A Year in the Wild

BPP

Contents

SPRING

Spring chorus.................... 12
Nest-building.................... 13
The trees awake................. 14
Growing up....................... 15
Hares are hopping.............. 16
Pond life.......................... 18
All in a row...................... 19
Butterflies & blossoms........ 20

SUMMER

In the meadow................... 24
Swallows swooping............. 26
Crickets chirping................ 27
In the reeds..................... 28
Glorious green leaves......... 30
Buds & bees..................... 31
Summer nights.................. 32

AUTUMN

Deer rutting..................... 36
Golden leaves................... 38
Dandelion clock................. 39
Time to fly...................... 40
Nuts & berries.................. 42
Forest fungi..................... 44

WINTER

Hibernation...................... 48
Bare branches.................. 50
Birds of a feather............. 52
Winter berries.................. 54
Robin redbreast................ 55
Red fox at night............... 56

A note from the artist........ 59
Glossary.......................... 60

Introduction

Life in the wild doesn't stay still for long.
Year after year, plants bloom in spring and fade
in autumn in a cycle as old as time. Animals follow
the pattern of the seasons too — searching for food and
rearing their young — sometimes passing many miles
between one chapter of their lives and the next.

Each section of this book uncovers the seasons'
changes, brought to life with hand-pressed plants.
You can see spring in the pearly pink of a petal, or see
autumn in the fiery red of fallen leaves. You can see
leaves, stems, even berries, all woven into the images.
All you need to do is look beyond the surface . . .

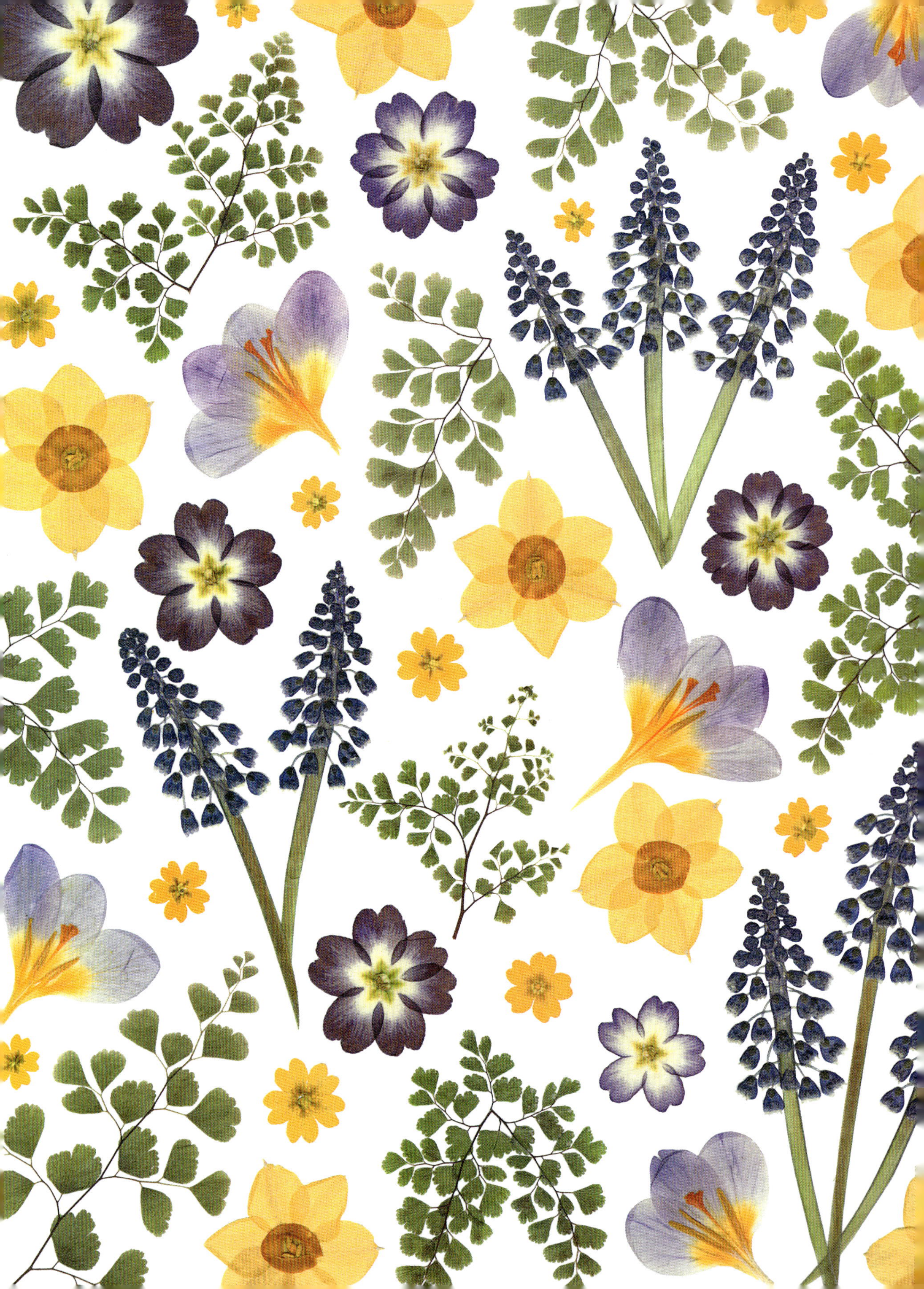

Spring

The winter frosts have melted and the long nights are growing shorter – spring has finally sprung. Snowdrops are the first flowers to rise, leading the way for more bright buds and blossoms. Chicks chirp in the trees, lambs frolic in the fields and tadpoles wriggle in the shallows. Everywhere you look there is new life: all just the beginning of an incredible year in the wild.

Spring

Spring chorus

The start of spring means just one thing for most birds. It's time to find a mate.

In the hour before dawn there is a flurry of birdsong: the dawn chorus is starting up. In this narrow window between night and day, the birds call out to each other, hoping to get noticed. The fittest males have the best odds of attracting a female as their song is the loudest and carries furthest.

As the sun rises higher in the sky, the birds then shift their attention to other matters. With more light to see by, it's time for them to go and find breakfast…

The blackbird is one of the first birds to sing each morning.

Spring

Nest-building

Look carefully in spring and you may see busy birds with beaks full of twigs, grass and moss – all the materials they need for nest-building.

Once a nest is complete and the eggs are laid, parents take turns sitting on them until the first chicks appear. If everything goes to plan there will be plenty of food for the chicks by the time they hatch – and they don't take long to start demanding food. Many birds lay their eggs so they hatch just as the first juicy caterpillars appear. This clever timing means they'll never have far to fly to gather food for their young.

Small birds usually lay one egg a day until they have a full nest.

The nest is woven from twigs then lined with soft moss or feathers.

Spring

The trees awake

After the long winter the trees are starting to show signs of change. Along their bare branches tiny green buds appear, then slowly burst open revealing the first new leaves of the year.

On other trees you can see fluffy catkins – hanging clusters of flowers whose pollen is carried in the wind. Their name comes from an old Dutch word for 'kitten', because they look like furry cats' tails!

Meanwhile the leafy stems of young ferns stretch upwards. Starting as tightly bound coils, their spiral shapes gradually open, unfurling to reveal a row of tiny fronds.

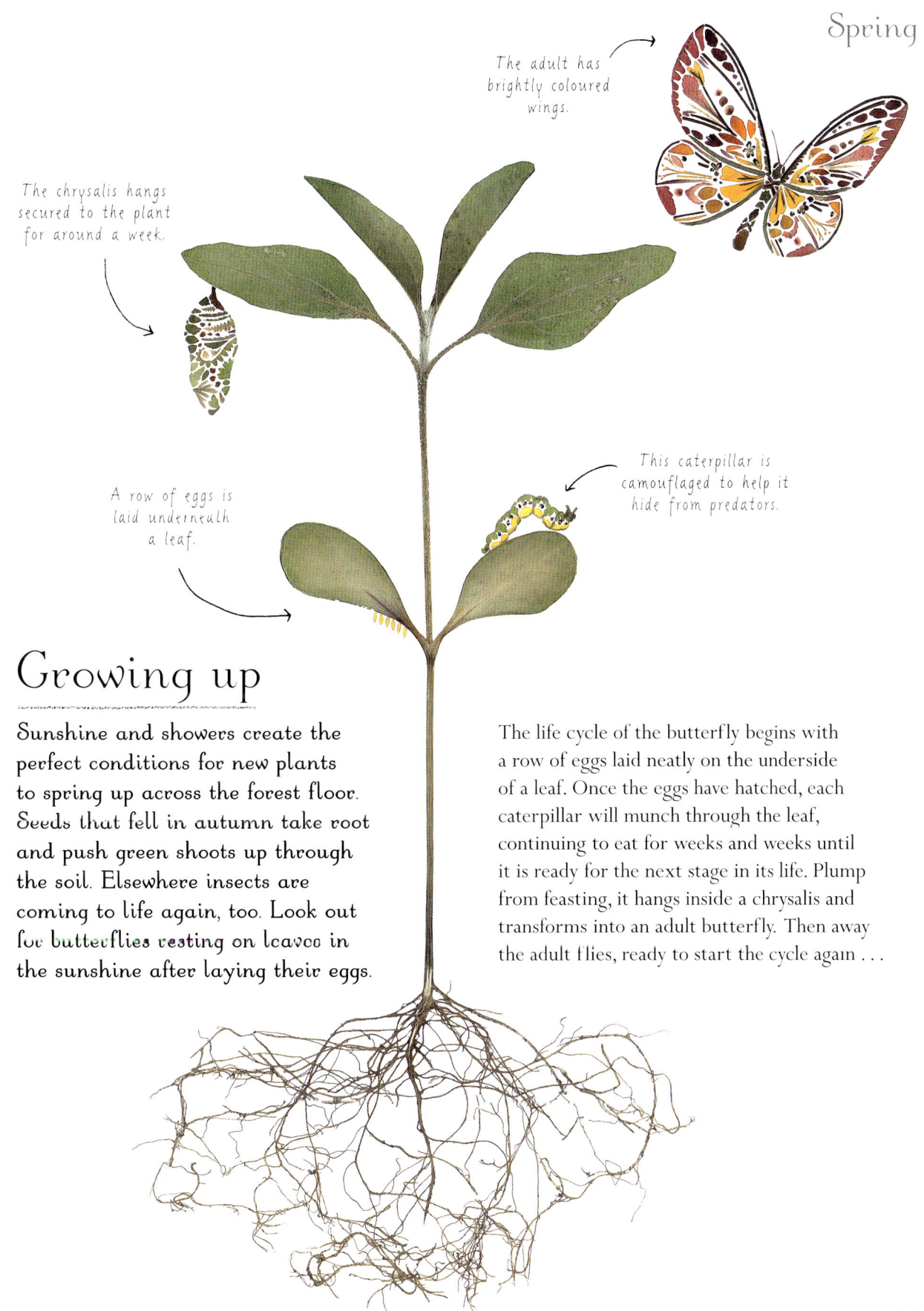

Spring

The adult has brightly coloured wings.

The chrysalis hangs secured to the plant for around a week.

This caterpillar is camouflaged to help it hide from predators.

A row of eggs is laid underneath a leaf.

Growing up

Sunshine and showers create the perfect conditions for new plants to spring up across the forest floor. Seeds that fell in autumn take root and push green shoots up through the soil. Elsewhere insects are coming to life again, too. Look out for butterflies resting on leaves in the sunshine after laying their eggs.

The life cycle of the butterfly begins with a row of eggs laid neatly on the underside of a leaf. Once the eggs have hatched, each caterpillar will munch through the leaf, continuing to eat for weeks and weeks until it is ready for the next stage in its life. Plump from feasting, it hangs inside a chrysalis and transforms into an adult butterfly. Then away the adult flies, ready to start the cycle again . . .

Hares are hopping

As the weather warms up, fields and meadows burst into life and hares can be seen darting through the long grass. Spotting a hare is a sure sign that spring has finally arrived.

This is the start of the hares' breeding season, when they can be seen 'boxing' in the fields. Females stand on their rear legs and beat off males, who try to impress a potential partner with displays of their strength.

With their long, lean legs and muscular bodies, hares are incredibly fast runners. They spend their lives above ground, sleeping in grassy nests. Their young, called leverets, are able to run almost as soon as they are born.

Spring

Hares are larger than rabbits, and can be identified by their long, black-tipped ears.

Look out for flattened patches of grass, which show that a hare has been in the area.

Pond life

Between the bulrushes at the edge of the pond, the water is teeming with activity.

Back at the start of spring, dozens of frogs arrived to mate and lay their eggs at the very pond where they were born. Now the jelly-like frogspawn is starting to hatch. Tiny black-headed tadpoles wriggle free then swim away, looking for weeds to nibble on and seeking shelter from predators, such as fish, newts and insects. In a few weeks they will grow legs and be ready to hop out of the water, just like their parents.

See if you can spot frogspawn, tadpoles and hopping adult frogs in springtime ponds.

Spring

All in a row

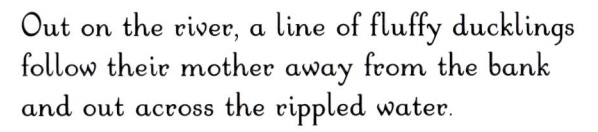

Out on the river, a line of fluffy ducklings follow their mother away from the bank and out across the rippled water.

Ducklings can swim almost as soon as they hatch, but their feathers are not quite waterproof yet. Until that moment comes they must stay close to their mother, as her waterproof oil rubs off on their feathers and helps them stay afloat. Meanwhile she keeps a watchful eye over her little ones.

Ducklings tend to swim in a long line, with the mother duck leading the way at the front.

19

Blossom is the name for the flowers of fruit trees, such as cherries, apples and peaches.

Spring

Butterflies & blossoms

A spring breeze blows, carrying with it a flurry of pink-white petals. They land, like snow, beneath the trees where butterflies flit between banks of bright flowers.

The warm days of late spring tempt more and more butterflies to appear. Some have made long journeys on their migrations while others are just coming out of hibernation. The spring flowers provide a rich source of nectar for the butterflies – just what they need after the winter. You'll see them most on calm sunny days, when neither wind nor rain can threaten their delicate wings.

Butterflies enjoy visiting flowers such as bluebells, crocuses and primroses.

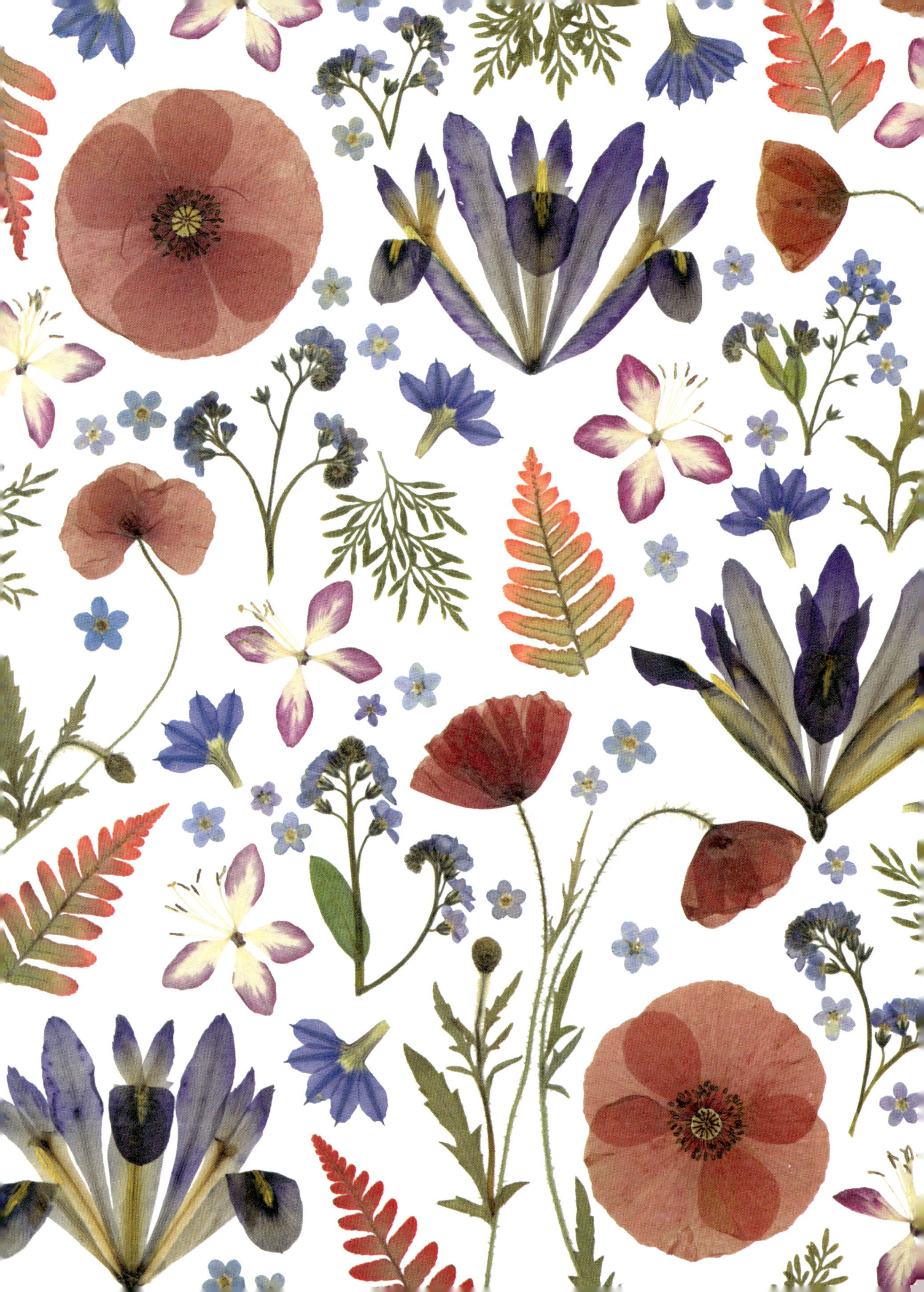

Summer

As the year approaches its longest day, the weather gets hot and wildlife thrives. Crowds of insects are a welcome meal for birds as they arrive from their long migrations. Young families born in the spring are getting bigger too, and you'll see them gradually venturing further from home. All this is set against a colourful backdrop of flowers — a summer showstopper perfect for attracting bees.

In the meadow

Out in the meadow, summer is in full swing – poppies sway in a gentle breeze and the crops turn golden in the sun. Meanwhile, nimble harvest mice climb the stalks in search of a mid-summer feast.

Since the wheat was sown in spring it has grown tall and strong, and now its heads are heavy with grain. At summer's end the crops will be harvested: the wheat grains will be ground into flour and its stalks will be dried to make straw.

Although harvest mice like to nibble crops, they also help farmers by eating insect pests.

Each harvest mouse nest is about the size of an orange.

Harvest mice are the only species of mouse to have flexible or 'prehensile' tails!

In the midst of the field, harvest mice scurry up and down the crops. They are agile climbers, using their flexible tails like safety ropes as they run and leap. It's a long way down but only up here will they find their favourite foods – berries, seeds and tasty crops such as wheat and corn.

Their neat, round nests are woven together from blades of grass and tucked up to a metre high between tall plants. Here their tiny babies will be safe from most predators.

Summer

Swallows swooping

Swifts and swallows fly with the seasons, following summer from place to place. Their fleeting visits are timed to make the most of the season's riches, as they gorge on all the insects they can catch.

At the start of summer, swifts and swallows arrive in their thousands, filling the skies as they pursue their prey of newly emerged insects. As their name suggests, they are remarkably fast flyers, diving and turning in mid-air, sometimes flying just inches above the ground. When not in flight, they can often be seen perching together in long lines along branches or power cables.

Swallows are able to fly for months at a time without landing.

Swallows can be identified by their long V-shaped tails.

Summer

Caterpillars can be seen munching on leaves all summer long.

Crickets have longer antennae than grasshoppers.

Crickets chirping

On hot, muggy days, insects seem to be everywhere and, though they can't always be seen, you're sure to hear the sounds of crickets and grasshoppers chirping in the undergrowth.

These long-legged insects make their courtship calls by rubbing their legs and wings together – and they're not the only insects in search of a mate. After spending years underground as larvae, stag beetles reach maturity in summer and males start looking for a female. They will only spend a few weeks in their adult form, so there is no time to waste.

Male stag beetles have large antlers, which they use for fighting rival males.

27

Summer

With their bright bodies, dragonflies are easy to spot as they zip between the reeds.

In the reeds

Along the water's edge the reed beds are full of activity. Flowers and grasses sway on their stalks, while ducks and moorhens hide their young families among the dense mass of stems.

Under the water's surface, the reeds also shelter young insects. Dragonfly larvae live underwater for up to two years, preying on tadpoles, fish and other insects. On sunny days the older larvae crawl out of the water and shed their skins, emerging as adults with colourful bodies and gauzy wings. The dragonflies must dry their wings in the sun before they can fly – but once they take to the air, they are one of the most formidable predators in the insect kingdom.

Irises and flowering grasses line the riverbank in summer.

*Summer*

Herons have long, sharp beaks for spearing fish.

Not only do the reeds provide shelter – they also provide camouflage for hunters like the heron. This lanky predator is perfectly suited to fishing in the shallows. It wades through the water on long legs, watching for fish with its keen yellow eyes. The moment it spots one, it will strike out with lightning speed, using its long neck and sharp beak like a spear to stab the fish then gulp it down in one.

Summer

Leaves clockwise from top: blackthorn, plane, elder, Japanese maple, black locust, field maple, English oak

Glorious green leaves

Spring's pale new leaves have reached full size and deepened in colour to a rich, dark green. Where the branches meet, they form a thick canopy over the forest floor and cast a little dappled shade against the summer sun.

Leaves are the lungs of a tree: it is here that air comes in and out of the plant, and that photosynthesis occurs – using energy from the sun to change carbon dioxide and water into energy-rich sugars. For deciduous trees, which shed their leaves in autumn and grow new ones in spring, summer is a time for growth and a chance to store up energy for winter.

Summer

Buds & bees

Summer is the season for flowers, and everywhere you look you'll see bright buds and buzzing bees.

The beautiful shapes, colours and scents of flowers make them favourites with gardeners – but more importantly, they mean the flowers attract bees and other insects. Flowers depend on these visitors to carry pollen from plant to plant so that they can grow new seeds. In exchange the insects are able to feed on the flowers' rich, sugary nectar.

Honeysuckle and bleeding heart flowers are known for their sweet nectar.

Bees buzz between forget-me-nots and violas.

Summer

Owls have wide, flat faces, which act like satellite dishes, directing tiny sounds towards their ears.

Summer

In some places you can see fireflies on dark summer nights.

Summer nights

As dusk settles into darkness, there are new faces to be seen: a band of nocturnal animals who come out at night to look for their prey.

Humid evenings are perfect for hunting. Earthworms wriggle to the soil's surface, rodents scurry through the undergrowth and the air is thick with flying insects – all ripe pickings for predators. Badgers and foxes, whose young are just old enough to fend for themselves, will eat whatever they can find, from beetles to birds. The owls swooping overhead are more particular, though. They glide silently, scanning the ground for a mouse to snatch up and carry away.

One badger can eat up to 200 earthworms in a single night.

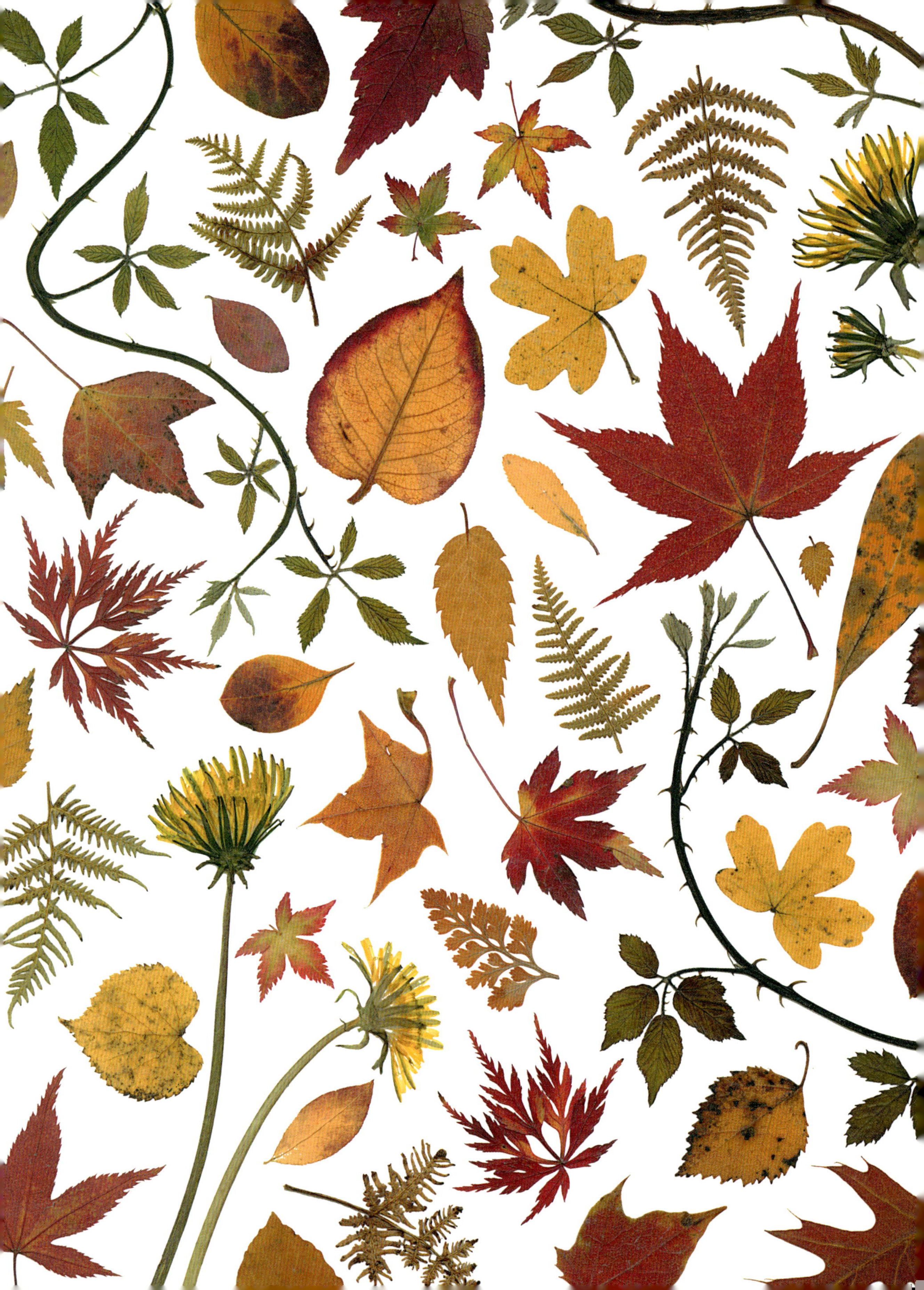

Autumn

The nights grow longer, the days grow cooler and the trees grow heavy with ripening fruit. Food is still plentiful, but all the signs show that winter is on its way. Animals hurry to make their preparations, tending to their burrows and gathering stores. They must fatten up before the cold season or else leave their summer homes and make their way towards warmer lands.

Deer rutting

As the sun rises and the autumn mists part, they reveal a great battle about to commence. It is the start of the annual deer rut when males compete for the right to mate — and competition is fierce.

Two stags eye each other from a distance, turning their heads to the side to fully take in their opponent. Then, with perfect timing the stags launch at each other, their bony antlers crashing together with a loud 'crack'. Each rival aims to get to higher ground and knock the other male off balance.

It is a long, drawn-out fight and a dangerous undertaking. Ruts can result in injury and even death, but the risk is well worth it. The winner will become the dominant male in the herd and have his pick of mates. At the end of the battle he bellows loudly to announce his victory. Unseen, the loser retreats into the mist. He will have to try his luck another time.

The 'crack' of antlers clashing together can be heard from over a kilometre away.

The larger male will usually win.

Autumn

Rutting stags often 'crown' themselves with bracken to make them look more intimidating.

Deer shed their antlers after the rut and grow a new pair over the spring and summer.

//Autumn//

Golden leaves

The woodlands put on a spectacular show as their leaves change colour, blazing with red, orange and yellow. Then the wind plucks and scatters them, making a crunchy carpet of leaves across the ground.

All summer long, deciduous trees have been soaking up the sunshine and using it to make food. But in the cold, dark winter, trees must save energy and protect themselves from frost and gales. The best way of doing this is by shedding their leaves.

First, the leaves stop producing the green pigment they use to photosynthesise and make food. As the pigment breaks down, it creates incredible autumn colours. Then, at last, the leaves fall off and drift away. From now until spring, the tree will survive on the food stores it made over summer.

Dandelion seeds have white, furry tufts to help them carry on the wind.

Dandelion clock

The autumn winds whisk away the fairy-like seeds of the dandelion plant, carrying them far and wide then letting them drop. They will grow wherever they land.

Often considered a weed by gardeners, dandelions can grow almost anywhere at almost any time of year. Their pointed, toothlike leaves are seen in most seasons, but even dandelions do not flower in winter.

Some people say you can tell the time by counting the breaths it takes to blow all the seeds off a dandelion head. This has led to their furry heads being nicknamed 'clocks'!

The name dandelion comes from the French 'dent de lion', meaning 'lion's tooth'.

Time to fly

As temperatures drop and food becomes scarce, many animals undertake a long migration to warmer regions. Clouds of butterflies drift towards the equator, whales follow the coast and some mammals start an epic overland trek. But perhaps the best known migrators of all are birds.

The sound of beating wings and echoing honks fill the skies as huge flocks leave their summer breeding grounds and head towards richer winter feeding grounds. Birds undertake some of the longest migrations in the animal kingdom, often following the same routes, known as 'flyways' or 'migration corridors', for generation after generation.

You can see large birds, such as ducks and geese flying in a distinctive V-shape, which allows the birds at the back of the flock to save energy. When the bird at the front of the group grows tired, another will take its place.

Autumn

Canada geese can be seen trailing across the sky in huge V-formations.

Listen out for noisy flocks of birds first thing in the morning and last thing before night.

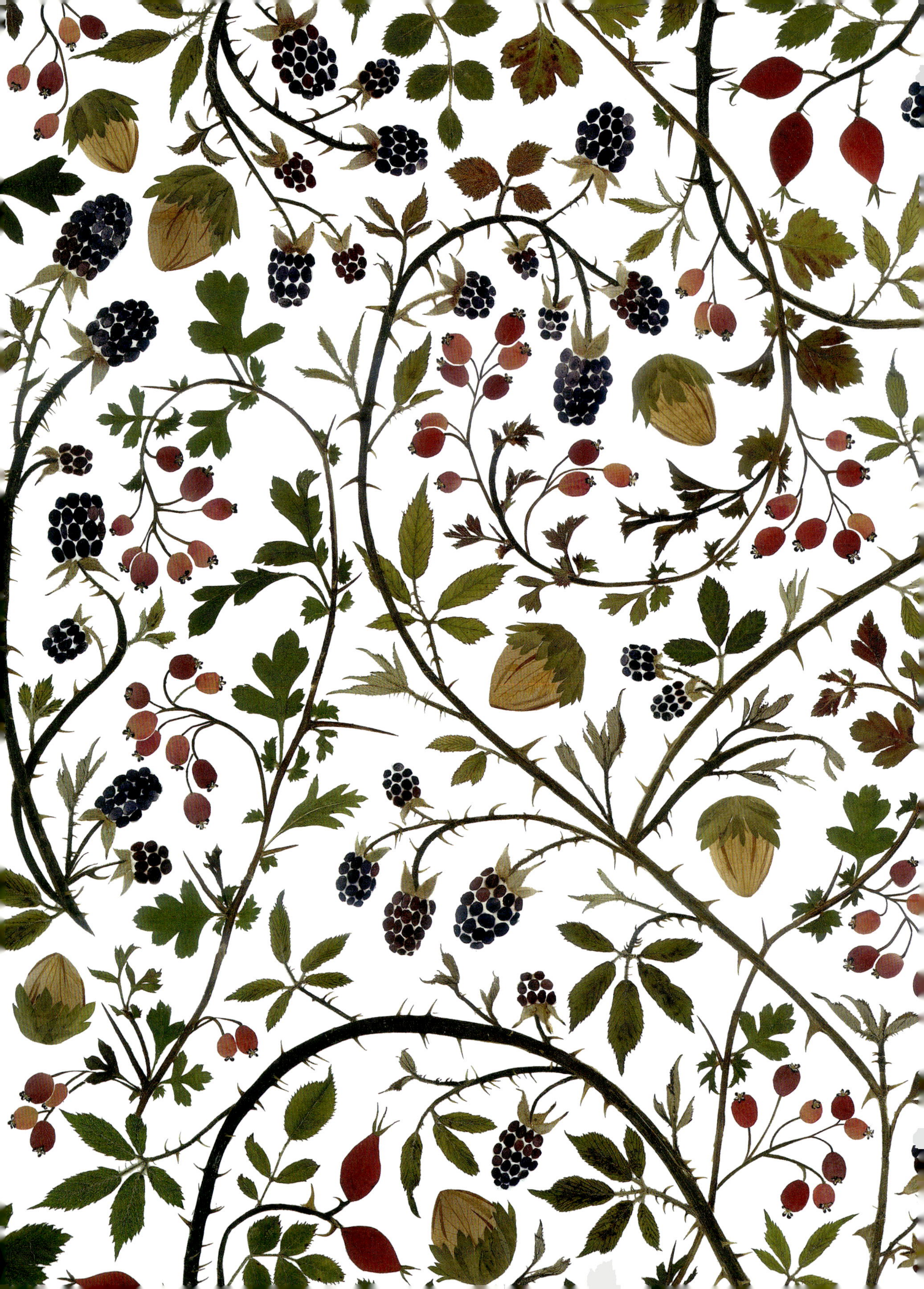

Autumn

Nuts & berries

Sweet fruits, juicy berries and hard-cased nuts hang like jewels among the hedgerow. These are the last fruits of the year before the onset of winter – and they are a feast for the animals that can reach them first.

Large animals such as deer and badgers gorge on fallen apples, while sharp-eyed birds peck the highest berries from the branches. Beneath the trees, bushy-tailed squirrels scamper back and forth, gathering nuts for their winter stores. Every year they do the same, burying nuts in the ground so they can return for them during the hungry weeks ahead. Most nuts will be dug up before spring, but any that are lost or forgotten could one day grow into trees.

Conkers have a hard, spiky case to cushion their fall and protect them from animals.

Autumn

Forest fungi

Autumn is the best time of year to see mushrooms and other fungi as they burst up across the forest floor in incredible shapes and vibrant colours.

A mushroom or toadstool is the only part of a fungus we can see. Most of it is completely hidden underground as an invisible web of threads winding through the soil. When the heavy autumn rains fall, they make fungi spring up above ground, revealing the part we call the fruit. Look out for fungi round the trunks of trees, along the edge of fields and growing in piles of autumn leaves.

While some fungi are safe to eat, many are poisonous. Only the most experienced experts can tell the difference between the two.

Autumn

Never pick and eat wild mushrooms — even if you think they look safe to eat.

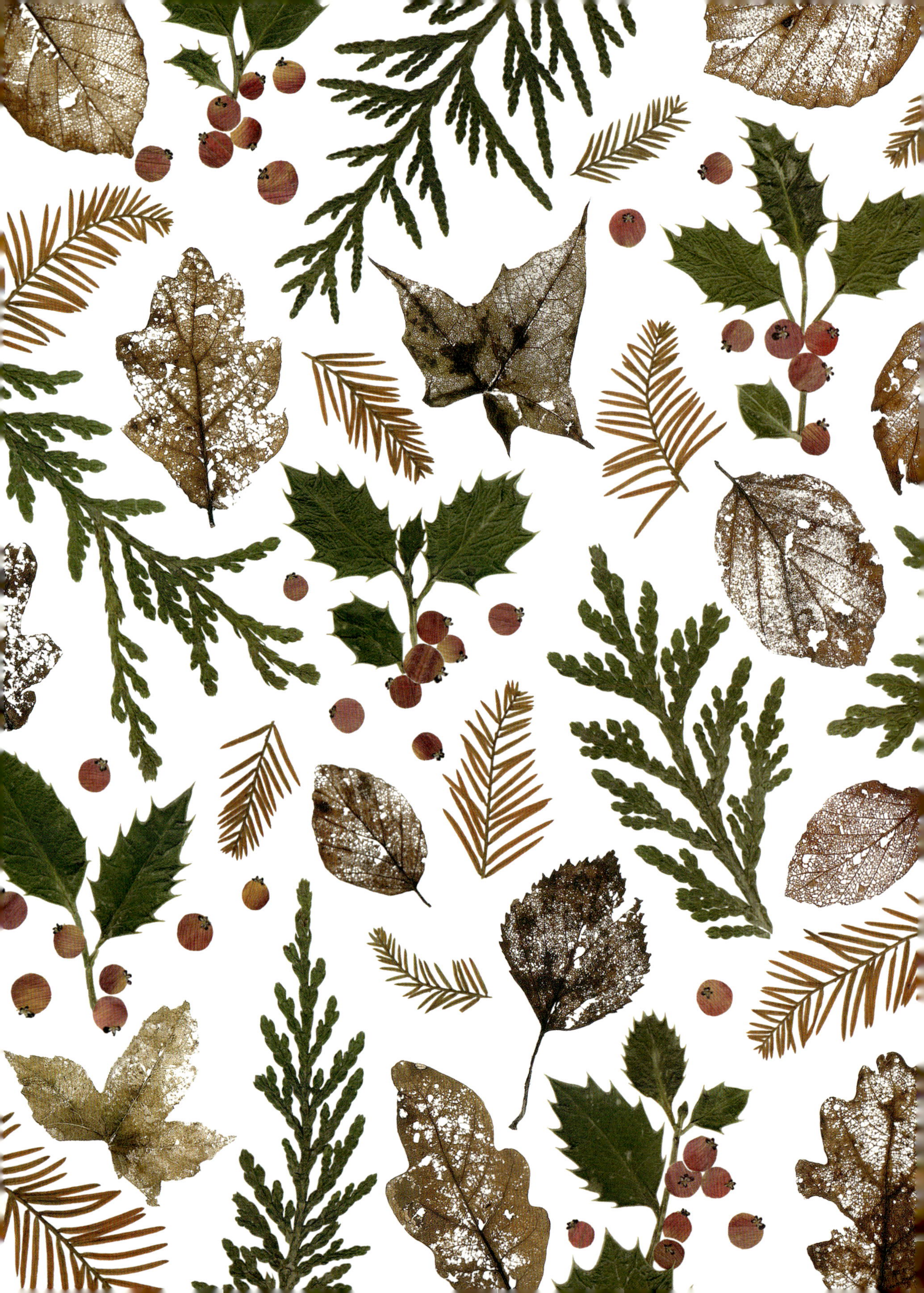

Winter

Winter can be a hard time in the wild. It is cold and dark, with frost and sometimes snow on the ground. Animals are scarce as many migrate or hibernate, and those that stay are tucked away inside shelters. But just look and you can still see signs of life, from frosted spiderwebs to paths of pawprints in the snow. Listen, too, and you will hear birdsong, even in the depths of winter.

Bats hibernate upside down in their roosts.

Hibernation

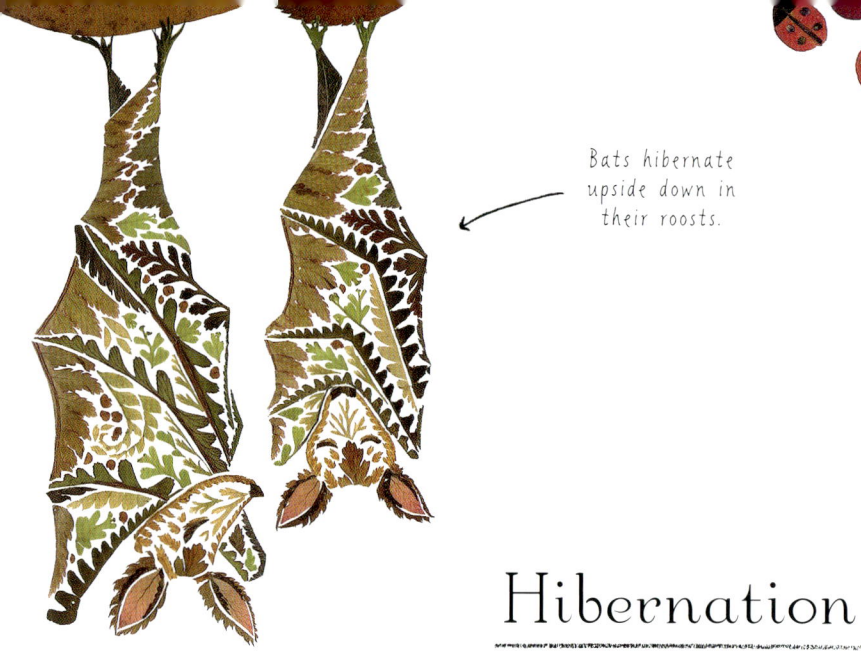

For some animals, the only way to survive winter is to go into a long, deep sleep called hibernation. During this time an animal does not eat, its body temperature drops and its heart rate slows right down, helping it to conserve energy.

Hibernating animals must eat as much as possible over summer and autumn, in order to build up their fat reserves. Then, as the weather gets colder, they will find somewhere safe to sleep: it needs to be sheltered from the worst of the winter weather and safe from predators. Small mammals such as mice and hedgehogs curl up in nests of leaves or burrows, while other animals look for shelter in caves, inside trees or tucked away underneath piles of logs.

Frogs burrow underground or hide among piles of logs to hibernate.

Ladybirds crowd together under bark or in rock crevices.

Winter

A hibernating hedgehog's heart rate drops from 190 beats per minute to 20, and its temperature falls to 10°C.

Winter

When leaves disintegrate they reveal the fine networks of veins that carry water around them.

Bare branches

The last of the leaves have been swept from the trees. Now their branches are still and bare, revealing their rough bark and twisting boughs — and sometimes even offering a glimpse of empty bird nests left over from spring.

While deciduous trees have lost their leaves, coniferous trees are still covered in green. Their thin needles have a waxy surface which prevents them from losing water and their leaves do not freeze in even the coldest weather. All this means they can keep making food right through the season, and keep their needles, too.

Winter

↗ Cypress

Coniferous trees, sometimes known as evergreens, grow their seeds in spiky cones. Some have spiky needles, while others have leaves like scales.

Juniper

Larch

Douglas fir

Spruce

Grand fir

51

Winter

Birds of a feather

Birds may have the option to take flight whenever they like, but winter is still a real test of their survival skills. Their main challenge is finding enough to eat, especially when snow and ice are covering the ground.

Many birds gather in groups, as huddling together provides warmth, and they can increase their chances of finding food by spreading out and searching further afield. With their thick layers of feathers, you are unlikely to see birds shivering from the cold, but you may notice some look particularly plump during winter. This is because they fluff air between their feathers to give them extra insulation.

Winter

Birds such as sparrows can be seen perched together along bare winter branches.

The smallest birds must eat around 30 per cent of their bodyweight every day in order to survive the winter.

Winter berries

In the coldest weeks, evergreen plants such as holly and ivy still thrive, and brightly coloured berries provide a welcome flash of winter colour.

Dense clumps of mistletoe hang high in the branches of other trees, where their pearly white berries are an attractive snack for passing birds. Other berries, like holly, are bright red, which makes them easy to spot. They are one of the few food sources available for birds during winter, but the berries need the birds just as much as the birds need them. Their seeds can only be dispersed if they are digested and then scattered in the birds' droppings.

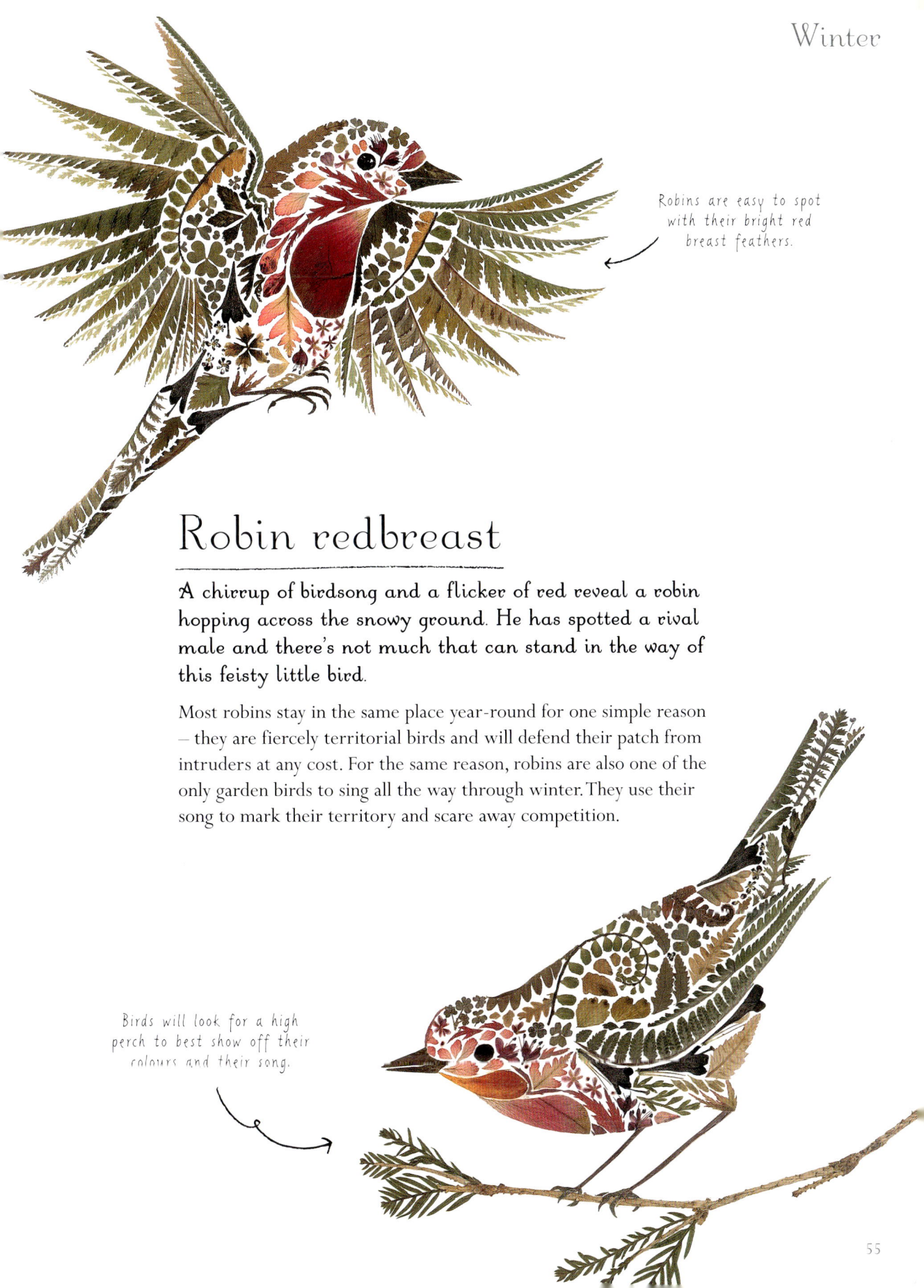

Winter

Robins are easy to spot with their bright red breast feathers.

Robin redbreast

A chirrup of birdsong and a flicker of red reveal a robin hopping across the snowy ground. He has spotted a rival male and there's not much that can stand in the way of this feisty little bird.

Most robins stay in the same place year-round for one simple reason – they are fiercely territorial birds and will defend their patch from intruders at any cost. For the same reason, robins are also one of the only garden birds to sing all the way through winter. They use their song to mark their territory and scare away competition.

Birds will look for a high perch to best show off their colours and their song.

Winter

Red fox at night

On a cold, frosty night a fox sets out, his paws crunching into the snow, ears alert to the slightest sound of movement.

Although the ground is covered in a sheet of white, the fox can hear tiny sounds beneath the snow's surface, and can pounce with great precision. His coat grows thicker in winter, and his bushy tail wraps around him like a blanket when he sleeps – keeping him snug on even the coldest nights.

When temperatures drop below freezing, water droplets freeze and turn to frost, coating everything in white.

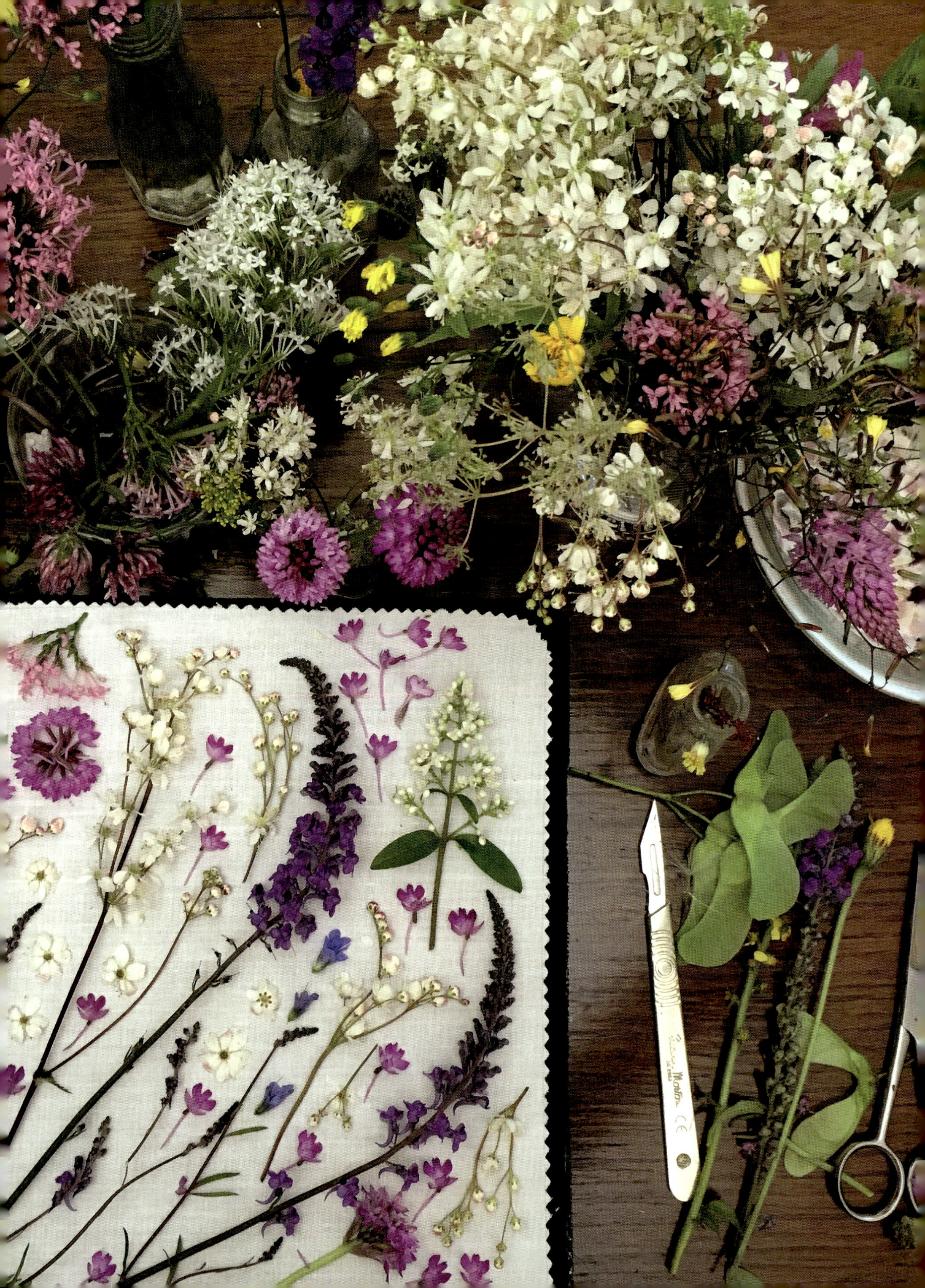

A note from the artist

Everything you see here – from the gleam in a fox's eye to the delicate line of a cobweb – is made from a plant. There is not a drop of paint in these pages.

Flowers and foliage are always changing with the seasons, but here they have been paused in their life cycle; kindled with a new story. Ferns are transformed into feathers and the colourful wings of insects are formed from the very flowers they feed on.

Each collage is made from hundreds of leaves and flowers, which are responsibly grown, or foraged in the wild, and preserved with traditional flower-pressing methods. The plants are then delicately arranged into bold new shapes and forms. They are all brimming with the twists and tangles of the wilderness, all capturing a perfect moment in time . . .

H. Ahpornsiri

Glossary

Camouflage
Colouring that blends in with an animal's surroundings and helps it to hide.

Chrysalis
A hard case inside which a caterpillar changes into a butterfly.

Coniferous trees
Trees also known as evergreens which have needles all year round and produce their seeds in cones.

Deciduous trees
Trees that shed their leaves in the autumn and grow new ones in spring.

Fungus
An organism that grows and feeds on decaying matter. Toadstools and mushrooms are both types of fungi.

Hibernation
A period of deep sleep some animals use to save energy and survive the winter.

Larva
A young insect before it develops into its adult form.

Migration
The movement of animals from one area to another, often following the seasons.

Nectar
A sugary liquid made by flowers and drunk by many insects and other animals. It is what bees use to make honey.

Nocturnal
An animal that is mostly active at night.

Photosynthesis
The process by which green plants use energy in sunlight to change carbon dioxide gas in the air and water from the soil into food for the plant to use.

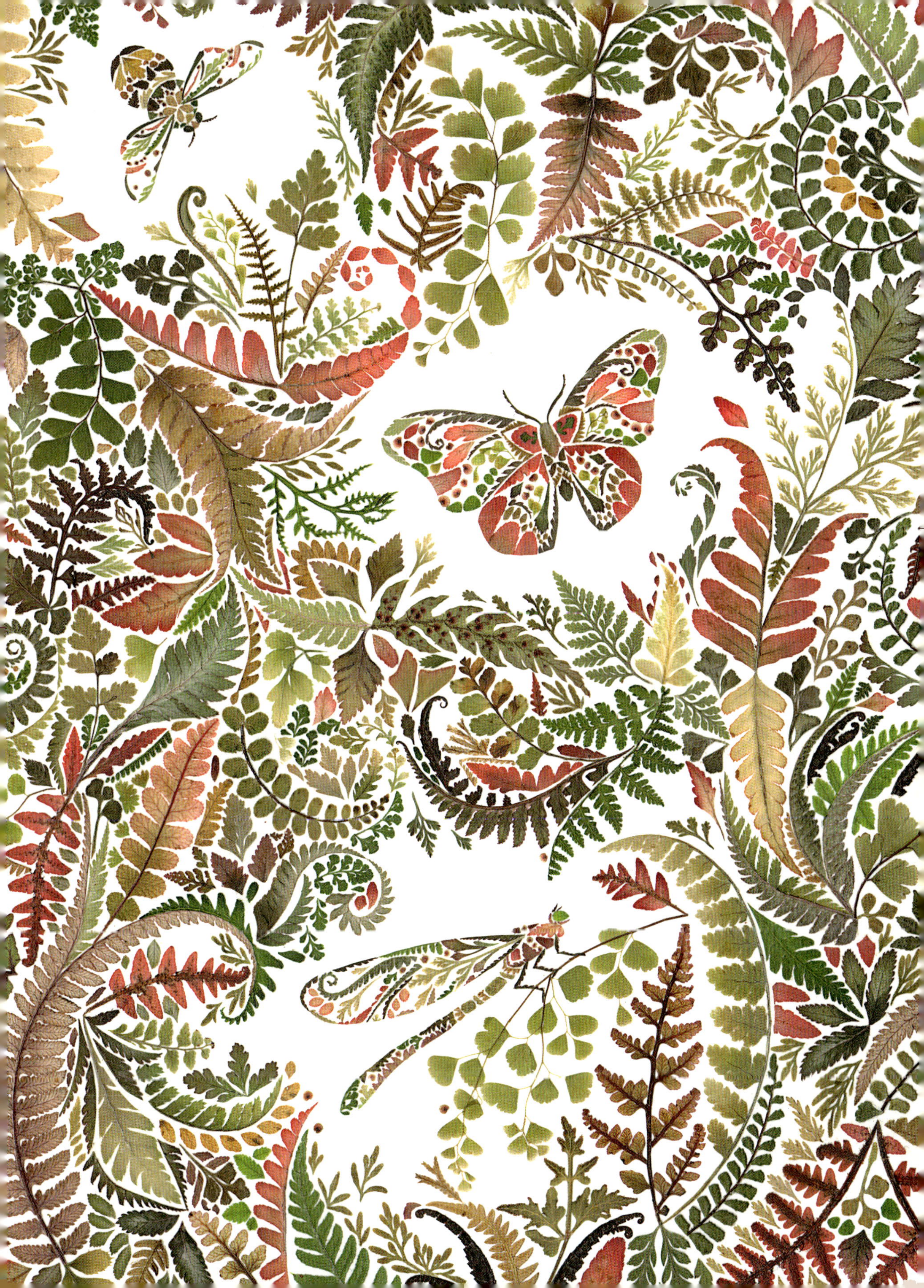

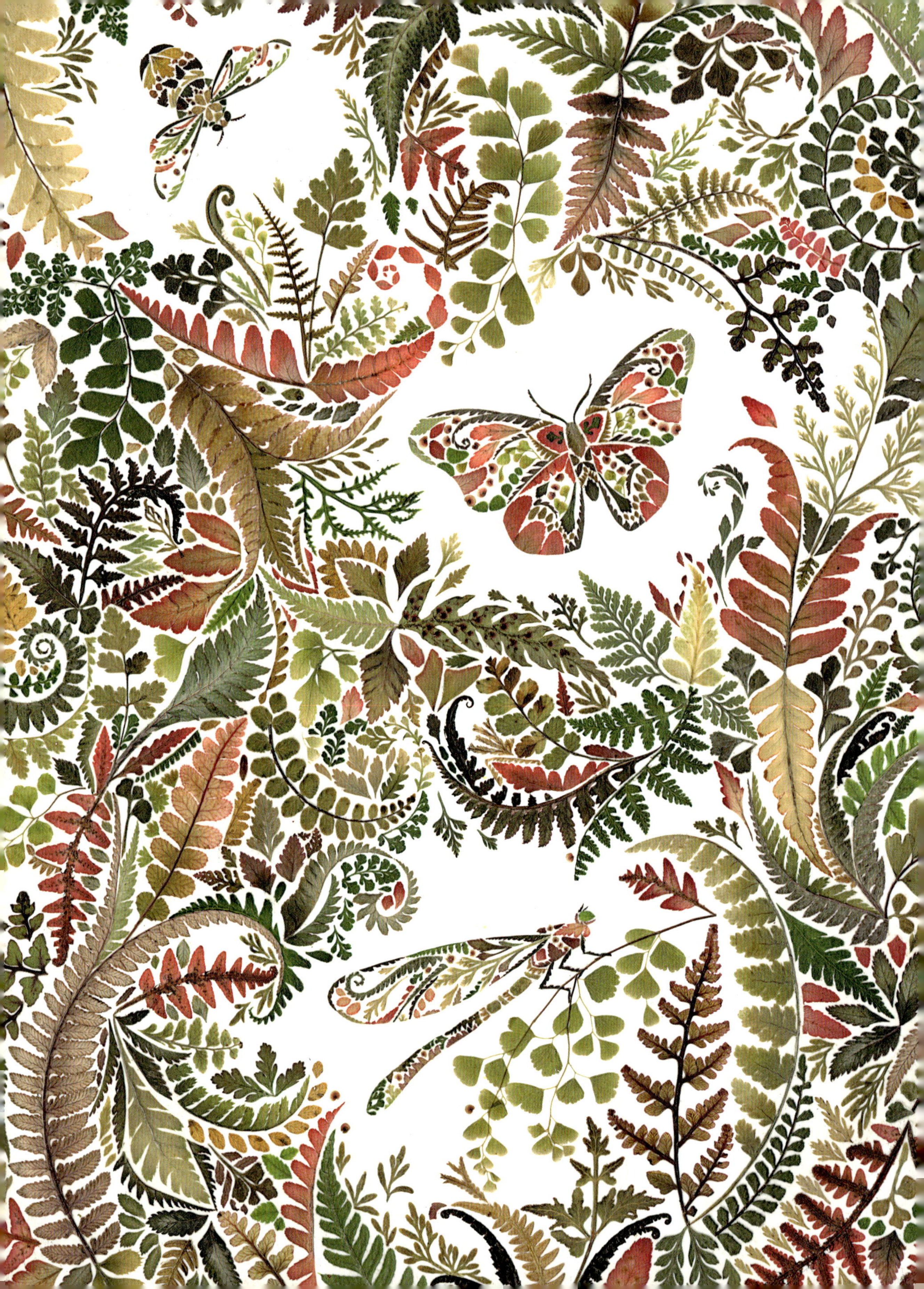